myBook 3

Authors and Advisors

Alma Flor Ada • Kylene Beers • F. Isabel Campoy
Joyce Armstrong Carroll • Nathan Clemens
Anne Cunningham • Martha C. Hougen
Elena Izquierdo • Carol Jago • Erik Palmer
Robert E. Probst • Shane Templeton • Julie Washington

Contributing Consultants

David Dockterman • Mindset Works®
Jill Eggleton

Printed in the U.S.A.

ISBN 978-0-544-45881-9

9 10 0868 27 26 25 24 23 22

4500845437 D E F G

myBook 3

Now You See It, Now You Don't

The Best Season
by Nina Crews

Celebrate America

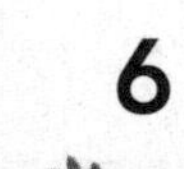

MODULE 5

Now You See It, Now You Don't

"Where there is sunshine, there is also shade."

—Kashmiri Proverb

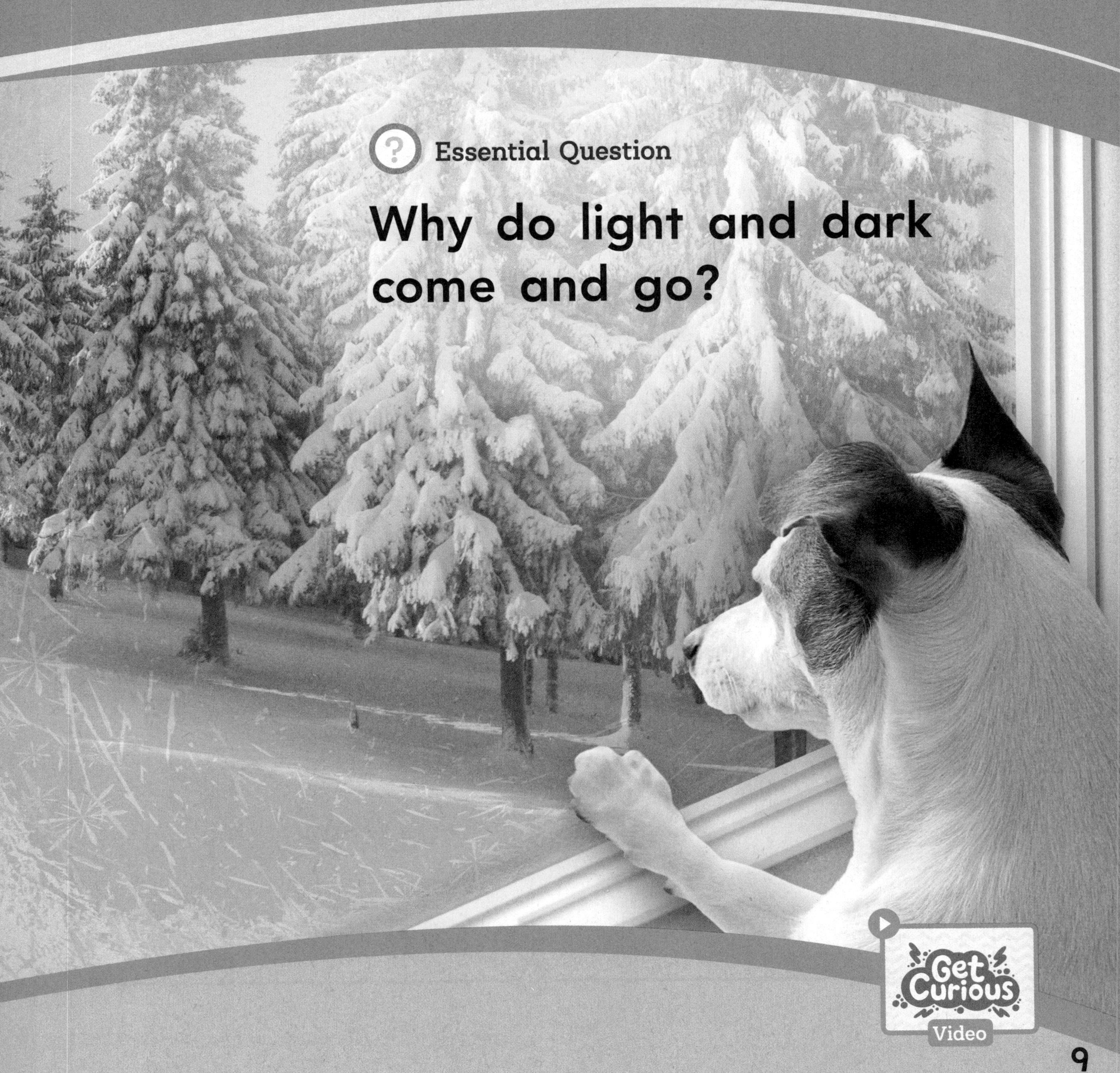
Essential Question
Why do light and dark come and go?
Get Curious
Video

Words About Light and Dark

Complete the Vocabulary Network to show what you know about the words.

solar

Meaning: If something is **solar**, it has to do with the sun.

Synonyms and Antonyms	Drawing

period

Meaning: A **period** is an amount of time.

Synonyms and Antonyms	Drawing

orbit

Meaning: When things **orbit**, they move around something in a circle.

Synonyms and Antonyms	Drawing

Short Read

READ Together

Super Shadows!

What is a shadow?

The sun shines and makes light.
Light goes through clear things,
like windows.
Light can't go through things
that are opaque.
You can't see through opaque
things, like you!
When something blocks light,
it makes a dark shape.

That's a shadow!

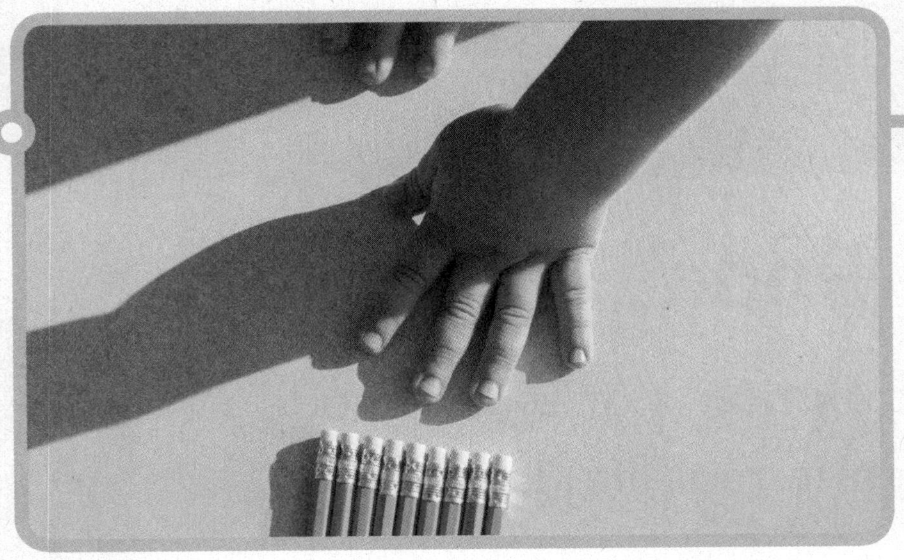

Fun Fact

Your shadow can be in front. Sometimes it is behind you!

Guided Practice

Prepare to Read

GENRE STUDY **Realistic fiction** stories are made up but could happen in real life. Look for:

- characters who act like real people
- events that could really happen
- places that seem real

SET A PURPOSE Read to make smart guesses, or **inferences**, about things the author does not say. Use what you already know and clues in the text and pictures to help you.

POWER WORDS
blackout
normal
busy
still
huddled
idea

Meet John Rocco.

BLACKOUT

BY JOHN ROCCO

It started out as a normal summer night.

The city was loud and hot.

AND THEN HE SAID...
TAP
TAP
TAP

INSIDE, EVERYONE WAS BUSY.

MUCH
sorry...

TOO

BUSY.

AND THEN...

THE LIGHTS

WENT

OUT.

All of them.

MOM!

NOTHING WORKED AT ALL.

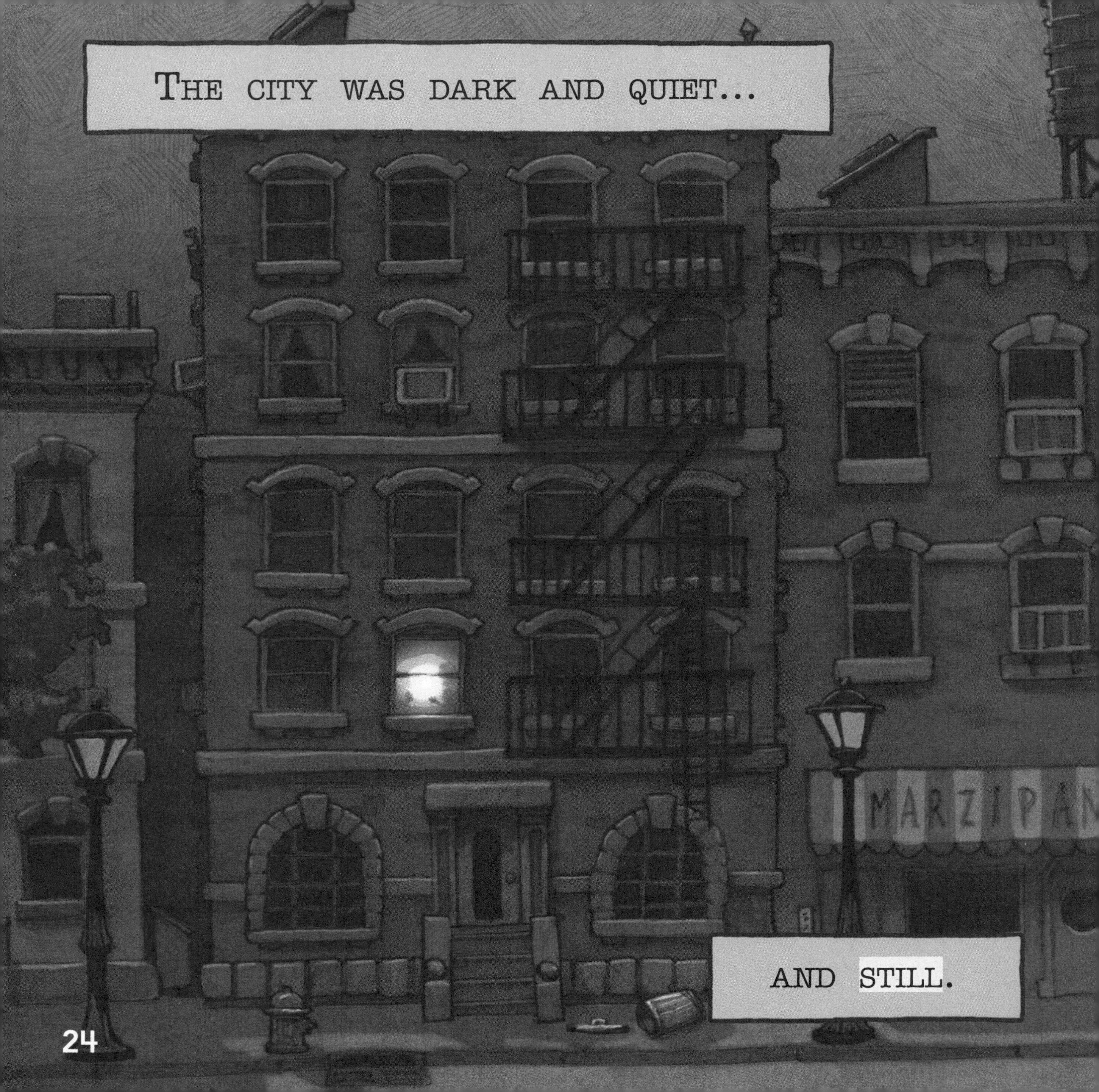

THE CITY WAS DARK AND QUIET...

AND STILL.

WE HUDDLED AROUND FLASHLIGHTS AND CANDLES...

...UNTIL IT WAS TOO HOT
AND STICKY TO SIT INSIDE.

SO WE WENT

UP

AND UP

AND UP

TO THE ROOFTOP AND FOUND...

THE LIGHTS.
AND PEOPLE!
IT WAS A BLOCK PARTY
IN THE SKY.

WE WAVED TO EVERYONE,
THEN HEARD OTHER SOUNDS BELOW.

SO WE WENT DOWN
AND DOWN
AND

TO THE STREET.

COME ON!

A PARTY WAS GOING ON THERE, TOO.

CREAM
FREE!
LA LA
LA
MARZIPAN'S
YIPPEE!

AND NO ONE WAS BUSY AT ALL.

WHEN THE LIGHTS CAME BACK ON,
EVERYTHING WENT BACK TO NORMAL...

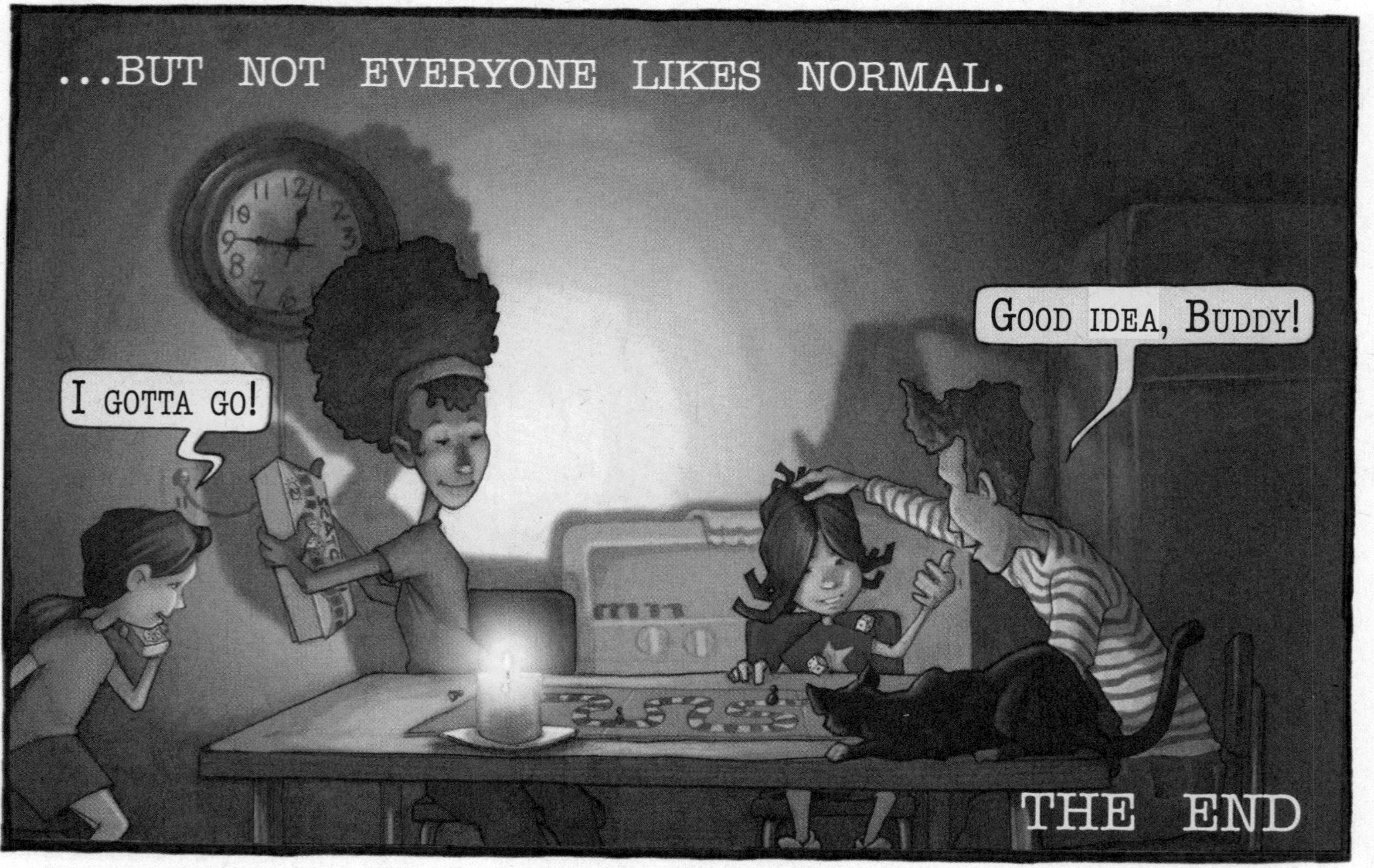

...BUT NOT EVERYONE LIKES NORMAL.

I GOTTA GO!

GOOD IDEA, BUDDY!

THE END

Use details from **Blackout** to answer these questions with a partner.

1. **Make Inferences** Do the characters care about each other? How can you tell?
2. Describe how and why a character's feelings change as the night passes.

Talking Tip

Complete the sentence to add your own idea to what others say.

My idea is ______________.

Cite Text Evidence

Write a Description

PROMPT How does the big sister change during **Blackout**? Why does she change? Use details from the words and pictures to explain.

PLAN First, draw what the boy's sister is like at the beginning and the end of the story.

Beginning

End

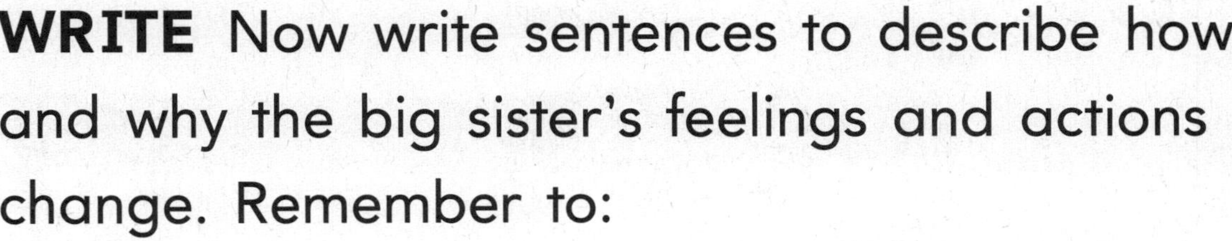

WRITE Now write sentences to describe how and why the big sister's feelings and actions change. Remember to:

- Tell what the sister says and does at the beginning and end of the story.
- Use describing words.

On My Own

Prepare to Read

GENRE STUDY **Realistic fiction** stories are made up but could happen in real life.

MAKE A PREDICTION Preview **Lin and the Stars**. You have learned that most stories include a problem. What problem do you think Lin has?

SET A PURPOSE Read to find out how Lin's problem gets resolved. Find out if your prediction is right.

Lin and the Stars

READ What is Lin's problem? Underline it.

Lin likes stars! She makes a paper telescope so that she can look at them. She will use it to see the stars in the sky. Lin is so excited!

That night, Lin looks up at the sky. Then she sobs and calls out to her dad. "I can not see the stars!" ▶

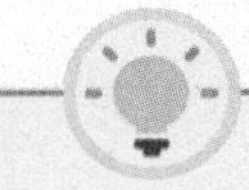

Close Reading Tip

Number the main events in order.

CHECK MY UNDERSTANDING

How does Lin feel when she can't see the stars? How do you know?

READ What solves the problem? Underline words that tell.

"There are many lights at night here in the city," Dad tells Lin. "The sky is not dark. You can not see stars here."

Lin asks her dad if they could camp out. Soon they go on a camping trip. The first night, they look up at the dark sky. Lin is surprised. "Look at all the stars, Dad! They are so beautiful! I am glad we could go camping. Thanks, Dad!"

Close Reading Tip

Mark important ideas with *.

CHECK MY UNDERSTANDING

Why can Lin and her dad see stars when they camp?

Cite Text Evidence

WRITE ABOUT IT Why do you think the author wrote **Lin and the Stars**? The author put a problem in the story. Why does having a problem in the story make it interesting to read?

Guided Practice

Prepare to Read

GENRE STUDY **Informational text** is nonfiction. It gives facts about a topic. Look for:

- headings that stand out
- diagrams with labels
- photographs

SET A PURPOSE Make a good guess, or **prediction**, about what the text will be about. Use the text features, like headings, to help you predict. Read to see if you are right. If not, make a new prediction.

POWER WORDS
faces
shines
fades
pattern

Build Background: Patterns in Nature

Day and Night

by Margaret Hall

Day or Night?

Look outside.
The sun lights the sky.
It is day.
But night is coming soon.
What makes day and night?

Earth spins, or rotates.
A full spin takes 24 hours,
or one whole day.
Day changes to night and
night to day as Earth spins.

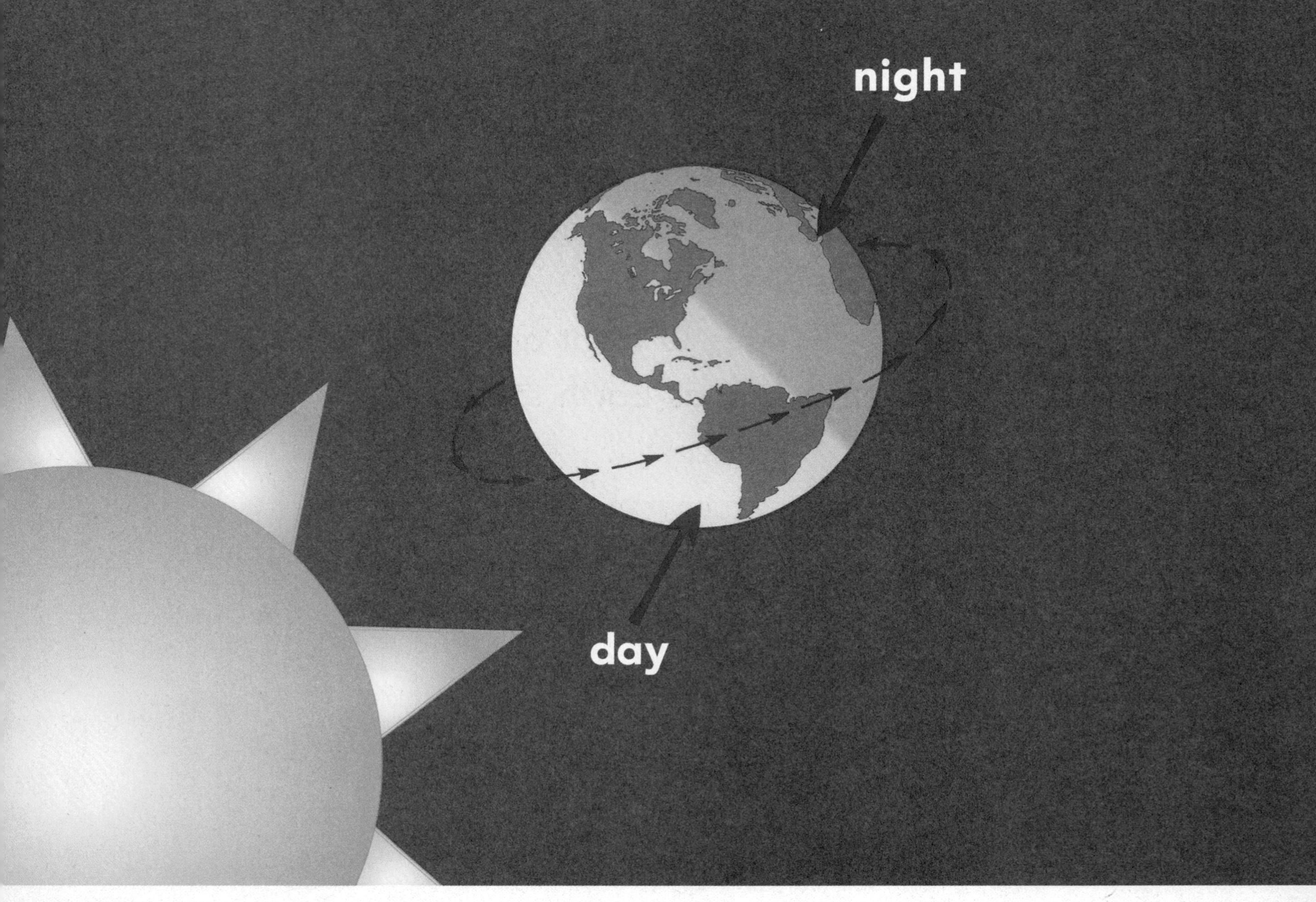

Part of Earth faces the sun.
That part has day.
The other side faces away from the sun.
It is night there.

It's Day

The sun shines highest in the sky at noon. Sunshine warms Earth during the day. Sunlight helps plants grow.

Earth keeps spinning.
The part of Earth that had
day turns away from the sun.
The light fades in the sky
as the sun sets.

It's Night

Now the sky is dark.
The moon and stars glow.
People turn on lights to help them see.
Night is longest in the winter.

Nocturnal animals hunt at night.
Owls can see mice in the dark.
Other animals sleep at night.

You sleep at night too.
Most people do.
When day comes again,
it's time to wake up.

It's a Pattern

Each day, the sun rises and sets. Night turning to day is a pattern. It happens again and again.

Use details from **Day and Night** to answer these questions with a partner.

1. **Make and Confirm Predictions** How did using the headings and other text features help you make predictions before and as you read? What were you right about? What was different?

2. How would things be different if we only had day and no night?

Listening Tip

Listen carefully. Think about what your partner is saying.

Cite Text Evidence

Write an Explanation

PROMPT Why do we have day and night? Use details from the words, photos, and diagram in **Day and Night** to explain.

PLAN First, draw pictures to show why we have day and night.

Why we have day:	→	Why we have night:

WRITE Now write sentences to explain why we have day and night. Remember to:

- Add describing words and details to make your facts clear.
- Tell information in an order that makes sense.

sun

Prepare to Read

GENRE STUDY **Informational text** is nonfiction. It gives facts about a topic.

MAKE A PREDICTION Preview **Rainbows**. Look at the text features, like the diagram, labels, headings, and photo, to help you predict. What do you think you will learn?

SET A PURPOSE Read to find out about rainbows and to see if your prediction is right. If not, use the text features to find and get information and to help you make a new prediction.

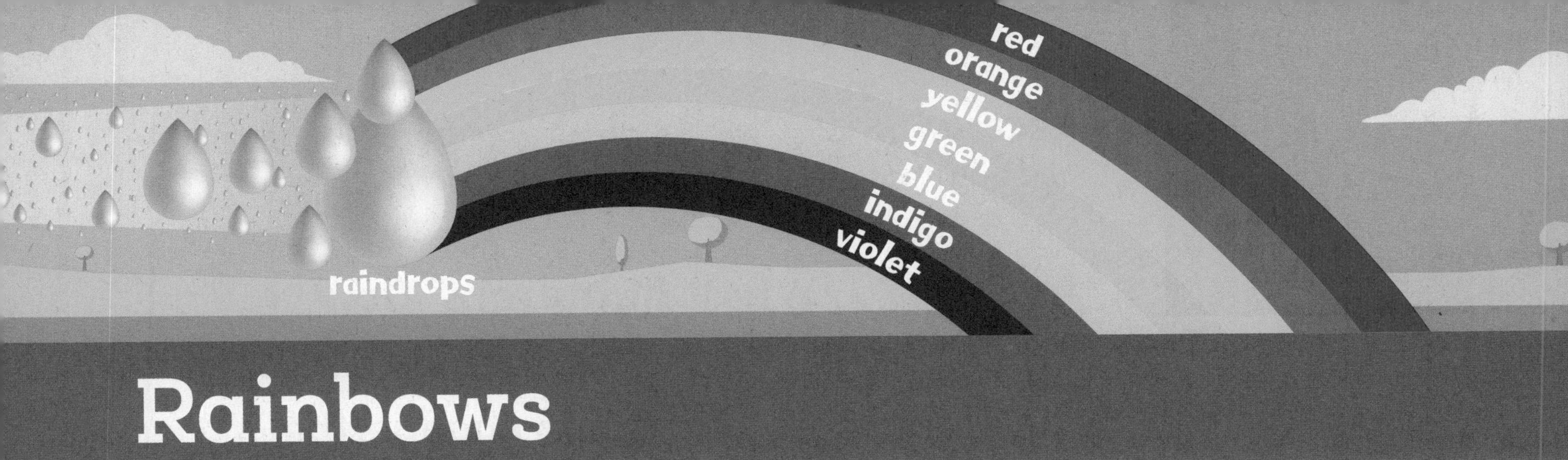

Rainbows

READ Underline the heading. What will this part be about?

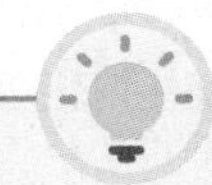

Close Reading Tip

Is your prediction right so far? If not, use the text features to help you make a new prediction.

Light Has Colors

You don't see a rainbow every day! You need sun and rain together to make a rainbow. Light from the sun is white. But it is made up of many colors! The colors are mixed together. ▶

CHECK MY UNDERSTANDING

What do you learn about light from the text and diagram?

READ Which part will be about raindrops? Underline the heading that tells. What do you learn?

Close Reading Tip

Mark important ideas with *.

What Raindrops Do

When the sun is out as it rains, it shines on the raindrops. The drops change the sunlight. They split the light into its colors.

A Rainbow Is Made!

Then you see red and blue. You see many colors in the sky. That's a rainbow!

CHECK MY UNDERSTANDING

Was your prediction from page 58 right? What were you surprised to learn about?

Cite Text Evidence

WRITE ABOUT IT Imagine that you are a raindrop! Write a letter to a friend. Tell how you helped make a rainbow. Use information from the text, diagram, and photo in **Rainbows** to explain.

Guided Practice

READ Together

Prepare to Read

GENRE STUDY **Opinion writing** tells an author's thoughts, beliefs, or ideas about a topic. Look for:

- reasons that support an opinion
- the word **because**, which tells you that a reason is being given

POWER WORDS
seasons
weather

SET A PURPOSE **Make connections** as you read. Find ways that this text is like things in your life and other texts you have read. This will help you understand and remember the text.

Meet Nina Crews.

The Best Season
by Nina Crews

A year has four seasons—winter, spring, summer, and fall. But which season is the best of all?

Winter is the **best** season. I love it!

I love winter because the weather is cold. Ice sparkles on the trees. The wind makes my nose cold. Cold winter days are great for ice-skating.

Winter is the best season because it snows! The snowflakes look pretty as they fall. Snow covers cars and houses and trees.

It is fun to sled. It is fun to make snowmen!

I like winter because it is a time to rest. Winter days are short. The sun sets early. Winter nights are perfect for hot chocolate and reading books. It is cozy and warm.

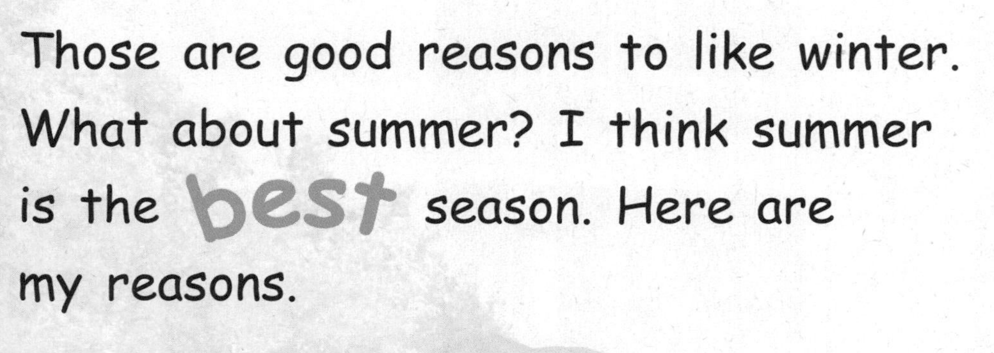

Those are good reasons to like winter. What about summer? I think summer is the **best** season. Here are my reasons.

Summer days are sunny. The sun makes flowers grow. Trees get leafy and green. Butterflies and birds fill the sky. Sunny days make me smile.

Summer days are beach days. The sand is hot. The water is cool. We can make sandcastles.

Summer days are outdoor days. There are many good games we can play. We can jump rope and play tag. Warm summer days are perfect for roller-skating.

I like summer because the days are long. Summer days slip into summer nights.

At sunset, the sky turns red. Fireflies dance in the air. It is fun to stay outside on summer nights. We can eat ice cream and strawberries. I just love summer days and summer nights!

Every season can be fun.

What is your favorite season?

Respond to Reading

Use details from **The Best Season** to answer these questions with a partner.

1. **Make Connections** How are **The Best Season** and **Day and Night** alike? How are the two texts different?

2. What is each girl in **The Best Season** trying to get you to agree with?

Listening Tip

You learn from others by listening carefully. Think about what your partner says and what you learn.

Cite Text Evidence

Write an Opinion

PROMPT Which person do you agree with in **The Best Season**? Use details from the text to explain why. What are your own reasons for liking that season?

PLAN First, write the season and reasons why you agree with the person you chose.

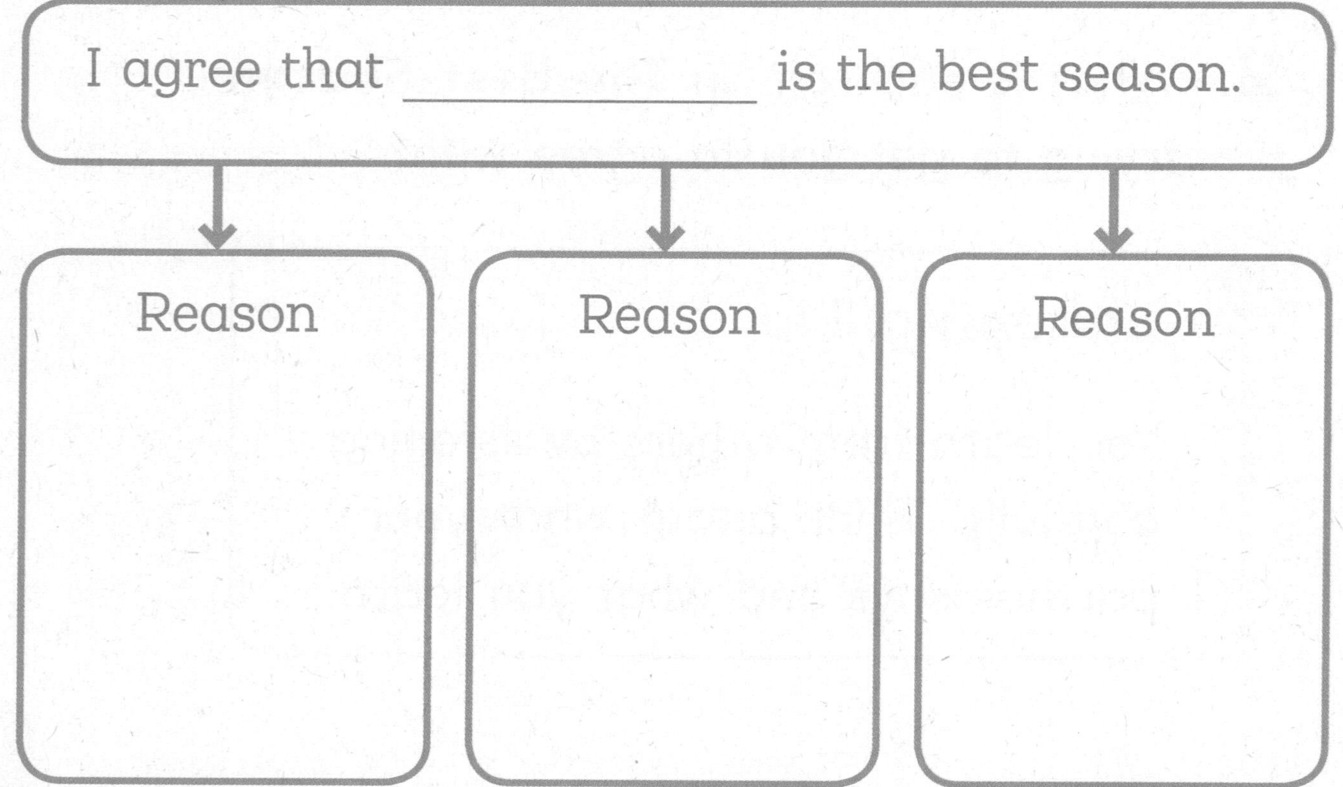

WRITE Now write sentences telling why you agree with the person. Then add your own reason for liking that season. Remember to:

- Tell your opinion.
- Use **because** when you write your reasons.

On My Own

Prepare to Read

GENRE STUDY **Opinion writing** tells an author's thoughts, beliefs, or ideas about a topic.

MAKE A PREDICTION Preview **My Great Town**. A boy likes the town where he lives. Why do you think he likes it?

SET A PURPOSE Read to find out why the boy thinks his town is great. Find out if your prediction is right.

My Great Town

READ What is the boy's opinion of his town? Underline it.

My town is a great place to live! I live here with my mom, dad, and big sister. There are fun things to do here in every season.

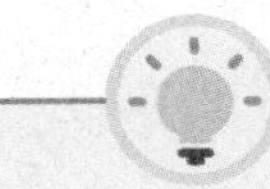

Close Reading Tip

Mark important ideas with *.

When it is hot, we swim. The water is cold, but I like it. I jump right in! ▶

CHECK MY UNDERSTANDING

The boy thinks his town is great because

READ What are more reasons the boy gives for why he likes his town? How does including many reasons in the text help you understand the boy's opinion?

Close Reading Tip
Write C when you make a connection.

In the fall, we go on hikes. We see all kinds of trees. The leaves are beautiful colors. When the weather is bad, we can go to the museum. I find out about animals that live around here, like bobcats. It is great!

Come to my town some day. You will see! It is a great place to live.

CHECK MY UNDERSTANDING

Why did the boy write this text?

Cite Text Evidence

WRITE ABOUT IT How is **My Great Town** the same as **The Best Season**? Use ideas from both texts to help you explain.

Prepare to Read

GENRE STUDY **Fantasy** stories have made-up events that could not really happen. Look for:

- animals that talk or act like people
- the beginning, middle, and end

SET A PURPOSE You learned that most stories include a problem. Use what you know about this text to make a good guess, or **prediction**, about the problem. Read to see if you are right. If not, make a new prediction.

POWER WORDS
wait
groan
worth
able
wasted

Meet Mo Willems.

Waiting Is Not Easy!

by Mo Willems

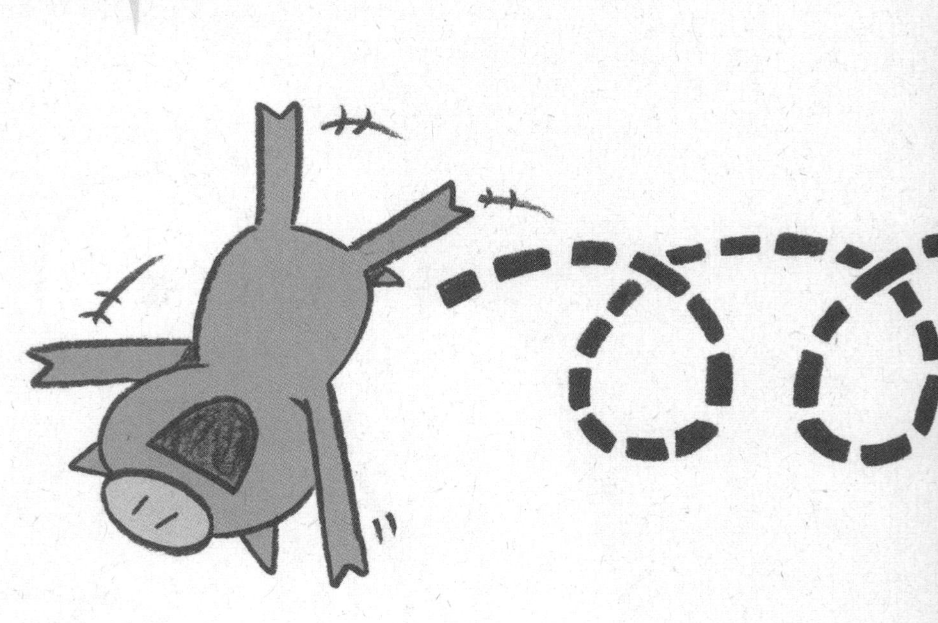
GERALD!

I have a *surprise* for you!

Yay!

What is it?

The surprise
is a *surprise*.

Oh.

Is it big?

Yes!

Is it pretty?

Yes!

Can we
share it?

Yes!

I CANNOT WAIT!

You will
have to.

Wait?
What?
Why?

The surprise is not here yet.

So I will have to…
wait for it?

Yes.

GROAN!
?

Oh, well. If I
have to wait,
I will wait.

I am waiting.

Waiting is not easy....

Piggie!
I want to see your surprise now!

I am sorry, Gerald.

But we must wait.

GROAN!
OOF!

I am *done* waiting!

I do not think your surprise is worth all this waiting!

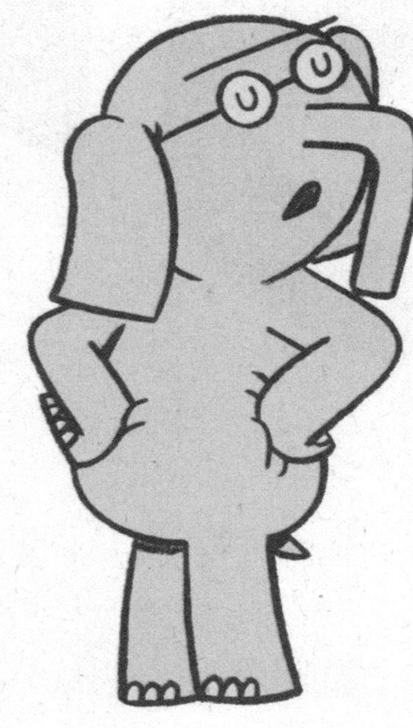

I will not wait anymore!
Okay. I will wait some more.
It will be worth it.

"

GROAN!
EEK!

Piggie!

We have waited too long!

It is getting dark!

It is getting darker!

Soon we will not
be able to see
each other!

Soon we will not
be able to see
anything!

WE HAVE WASTED
THE WHOLE DAY!

Well...
Um...

We have waited and waited and waited and waited and waited!

And for WHAT!?

This was worth the wait.

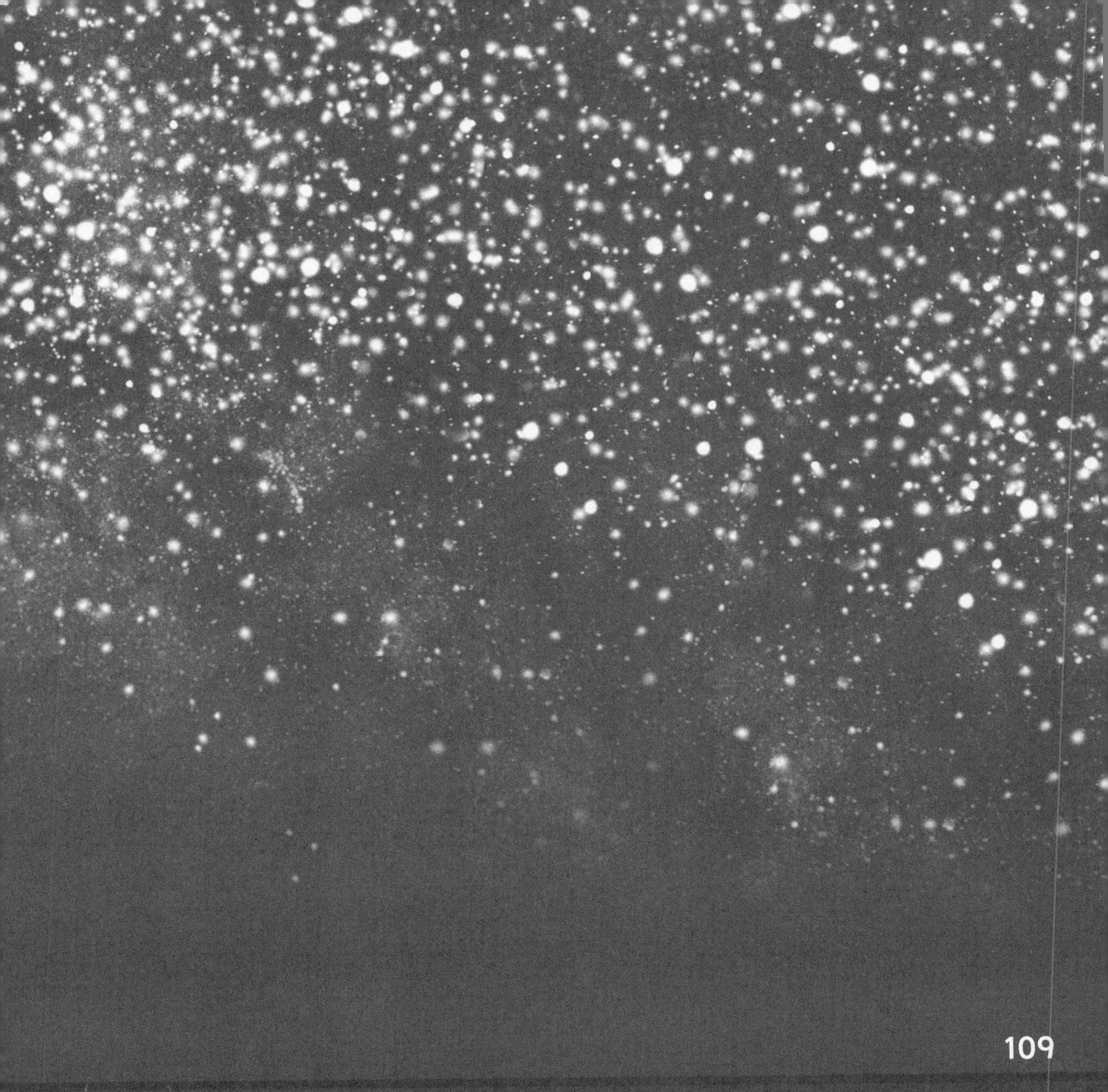

Tomorrow morning I want to show you the sunrise.
I cannot wait.

Use details from **Waiting Is Not Easy!** to answer these questions with a partner.

1. **Make and Confirm Predictions** Tell about predictions you made about the story's problem and resolution before and as you read. What were you right about? What was different in the story?

2. How does Gerald feel about waiting? Tell how you know.

Listening Tip

Listen carefully. Think of questions to ask your partner to find out more.

Cite Text Evidence

Write a Riddle

PROMPT Pick Gerald or Piggie. Use details from **Waiting Is Not Easy!** to write clues that describe the character. Use these clues to write your own riddle!

PLAN First, tell what the character is like.

Says	Does	Looks Like

WRITE Now write your clues in sentences. Don't tell the character's name. End with a question, like **Who am I?** Remember to:

- Describe what the character says, does, and looks like.
- Use a question mark **(?)** to end a question.

Prepare to Read

GENRE STUDY **Fantasy** stories have made-up events that could not really happen.

MAKE A PREDICTION Preview **Liz's Shadow**. You have learned that most stories are set up the same way—there is a problem to solve. What do you think the problem is in this story?

SET A PURPOSE Read to find out if Liz's problem gets solved and to see if your prediction is right. If not, think about the story's problem and make a new prediction as you read.

Liz's Shadow

READ What does Liz want to know? Underline words that tell.

One day, Liz saw that her shadow was long in the morning but short at lunch. "Why did my shadow change size?" she said. Just then, she saw Q-BOT fly by! Q-BOT is a hero who helps all kids who want to know more. Liz asked Q-BOT to help her. ▶

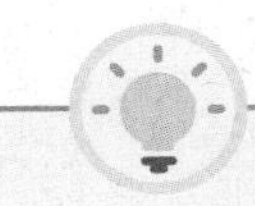

Close Reading Tip

Circle words you don't know. Then figure them out.

CHECK MY UNDERSTANDING

Describe what Q-BOT is like.

READ Was your prediction on page 114 right? If not, make a new prediction about what Liz's problem is and how it will get solved. Read on to find out what happens.

Close Reading Tip

Mark important ideas with *.

"Put on your jet pack!" said Q-BOT. In a flash, they were out in space. "Look at Earth. It spins!" Q-BOT said. "On Earth, it looks like the sun rises and sets. In the morning, the sun is low. Your shadow is long. At lunch, the sun is up high. Your shadow is short. Later, the sun goes down low. Your shadow is long again."

"It was fun to find out about shadows!" said Liz. "Now, what are stars like?"

CHECK MY UNDERSTANDING

What lesson does Liz learn from being with Q-BOT?

Cite Text Evidence

WRITE ABOUT IT To help you make predictions, you used what you know about the story's problem and how it could be solved. Did your predictions match what happened? Write to tell what you were right about. Also, tell what happened differently.

Guided Practice

READ Together

Prepare to View

GENRE STUDY **Songs** are words set to music. We can sing them out loud. Listen for:

- information about the topic
- the ways words and sounds work together
- musical notes, words, and phrases that give the song rhythm

SET A PURPOSE Listen to the song to find out the **central idea**, or main thing the song is about. Look and listen for important details that help you understand the central idea.

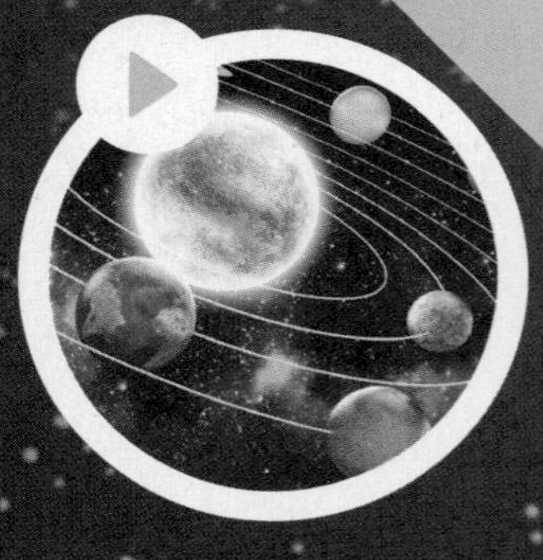

Build Background: The Solar System

I'M SO HOT

from StoryBots

As You View Watch to find out what the sun is like. What different things does the sun do? Think as you watch. What is the main thing this video is showing you about the sun? Use details in the song and the pictures to figure out this central idea.

Use details from **I'm So Hot** to answer these questions with a partner.

1. **Central Idea** What is the main thing, or central idea, the video teaches about the sun? What are some details in the video that help explain this central idea?

2. Describe what the sun is like.

Listening Tip

Listen carefully. Think about what your partner is telling you about the topic.

Let's Wrap Up!

Essential Question

Why do light and dark come and go?

Pick one of these activities to show what you have learned about the topic.

1. **Be a Poet**

You have read about light and dark, day and night, and the seasons. Write a poem that includes information you have learned. Draw a picture to go with it. Share your poem with your class!

2. Day and Night Face-Off

Your opinion counts! Do you like day or night better? Find facts to explain your ideas. Then tell a partner your opinion and explain why.

Word Challenge

Can you use the word solar to help explain your opinion?

My Notes

MODULE 6

Celebrate America

"The history of every country begins in the heart of a man or a woman."

—Willa Cather

Essential Question

What do holidays and symbols tell about our country?

READ Together

Words About Holidays and Symbols

Complete the Vocabulary Network to show what you know about the words.

participate

Meaning: When you **participate**, you take part in doing something.

Synonyms and Antonyms	Drawing

duty

Meaning: A **duty** is something that you should do.

Synonyms and Antonyms	Drawing

appreciate

Meaning: When you **appreciate** something, you are thankful for it.

Synonyms and Antonyms	Drawing

Short Read

READ Together

State the Facts!

What do you know about your state? Do some research. Get the facts! Check out these facts.

I live in Texas. It is a big state! Our state flag is red, white, and blue with a big star. The state flower is the bluebonnet.

Texas

I'm from Florida. Our state reptile is the alligator! The sabal palm is the state tree. These trees can grow 80 feet tall!

I live in Virginia. The dogwood is our state tree. It has flowers in the spring and red berries in the fall. The cardinal is our state bird.

Virginia

Florida

Guided Practice

READ Together

Prepare to Read

GENRE STUDY **Dramas** are stories that are read and acted out. Look for:

- settings where the story takes place
- a narrator who says words the characters do not say

SET A PURPOSE Make a good guess, or **prediction**, about what will happen. Use the characteristics of drama, such as characters and settings, to help you. Read to see if you are right. If not, make a new prediction.

POWER WORDS
scene
monuments
sights
grouchy
freedom
symbol

Meet Jerdine Nolen.

Monument City

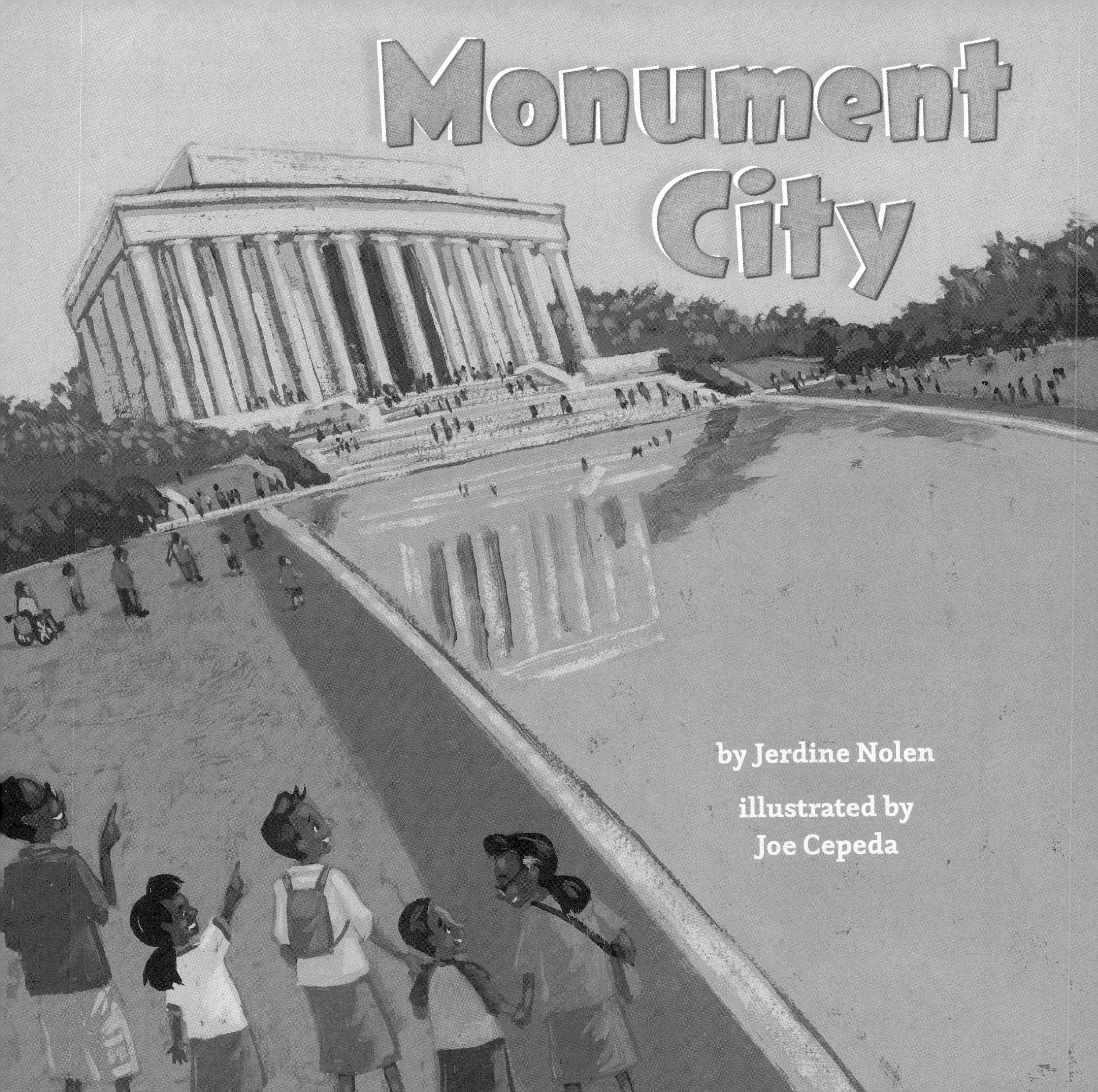

by Jerdine Nolen

illustrated by Joe Cepeda

CAST
DAD
MOM
JEFF
DEB
GRANDMA
NARRATOR
JULY
4

Scene 1: Good News

NARRATOR: One morning, Mom and Dad had some good news.

MOM: We are going on a family trip to Washington, D.C., next week!

JEFF: Does it have a water park, Mom?

MOM: I don't know. I know it has a big river.

DEB: The Potomac River.

JEFF: Well, what can we do there for fun?
MOM: Washington, D.C., has lots of great monuments. Some are very big!
DEB: We will see all the sights!

DAD: We will stay with Grandma. She lives near the city.

DEB: Perfect! We will be there for the Fourth of July!

JEFF: But I want to go to a water park on the Fourth of July!

Scene 2: The White House

NARRATOR: The family went to Washington, D.C., and met Grandma at the White House.

JEFF: What is so great about a house that is white?

DAD: Just wait and see.

DEB: I see Grandma!

JEFF: Why are so many people here?

GRANDMA: Oh, honey, everyone wants to see the White House. It is the president's house.

JEFF: The president lives here?

DEB: Yes, the First Family lives here.

GRANDMA: The White House has 35 bathrooms and 132 rooms.

DEB: If I lived here, I could have my own bathroom.

JEFF: So could I!

Scene 3: The Capitol

NARRATOR: The family went to see the Capitol.

DAD: What do you think of the Capitol, kids?

JEFF: Oh, no, Dad! Not *another* building.

DEB: Stop being so grouchy, Jeff!

DEB: This is where laws are made.
JEFF: What is that up on the top?
GRANDMA: That is the Statue of Freedom.
DAD: It is a symbol of our country's freedom.

JEFF: What is that tall thing way over there?
MOM: It is named after our first president.
JEFF: George Washington!
DAD: Very good! Tomorrow we will go to the very top.
JEFF: We will? How many steps does it have?
DAD: 897!

Scene 4: The Washington Monument

DEB: The Washington Monument is the tallest monument in the city.

JEFF: It has 897 steps, but we don't walk up. We take an elevator. It takes one minute to get to the top.

GRANDMA: You kids know as much about this city as I do!

GRANDMA: The next monument we will see is over there. It honors our 16th president.

DEB: Abraham Lincoln.

Scene 5: The Lincoln Memorial

GRANDMA: If the statue inside could stand up, it would be 28 feet tall.

DEB: Mom, do you have a penny? My teacher said the Lincoln Memorial is on the back of some pennies.

JEFF: Let me see that!

DAD: Kids, walk down to step number 18 with me.

JEFF and **DEB:** One, two, three . . .

DAD: Take a good look when we get to step 18.

DEB: Why do you want us to stand here, Dad?
DAD: Remember this step. I will tell you why when we get to the next monument.
JEFF: *Another* one?

Scene 6: The Martin Luther King, Jr. Memorial

GRANDMA: The monument to honor Dr. Martin Luther King, Jr. is one of our newest monuments.

JEFF: He looks like he could walk right out of that rock!

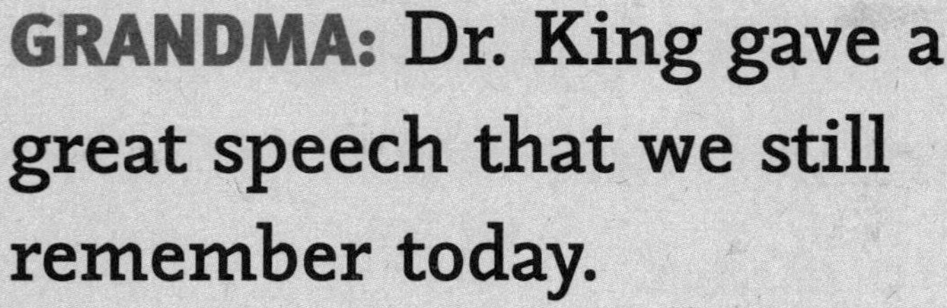

GRANDMA: Dr. King gave a great speech that we still remember today.

MOM: It was the "I Have a Dream" speech.

JEFF: My teacher read it to us. We made a picture about our dreams.

DEB: In school, we honor Dr. King on his birthday.

DAD: Do you remember which step we were on?

JEFF: 18!

DAD: Yes! That is the step Dr. King was on when he gave his speech.

MOM: Many, many people came to listen to him.

GRANDMA: I was one of those people.

Scene 7: The Fourth of July

NARRATOR: Jeff's cousin and family are going to a water park for Fourth of July. Jeff wants to go with them.

JEFF: I don't know what to do!

MOM: It is up to you, Jeff.

GRANDMA: You can't miss the Fourth of July in Washington, D.C.! It is our country's birthday. We are all invited to the party!

DEB: Will there be marching bands?

GRANDMA: You bet! And when the stars come out, we will listen to music . . .

DEB: . . . and watch the fireworks!

JEFF: Then I want to go!

JEFF: Happy Fourth of July!

Use details from **Monument City** to answer these questions with a partner.

1. **Make and Confirm Predictions** Tell about predictions you made using the characteristics of drama, such as settings. What were you right about? What happened differently in the drama?

2. Why is Washington, D.C., an important place?

Talking Tip

Your ideas are important! Speak loudly and clearly to share them.

Cite Text Evidence

Write a Drama

PROMPT Pick a scene from **Monument City**. Rewrite it your own way as a short drama. Add yourself as a character. Then share your drama with classmates. Tell them what things about your writing make it a drama.

PLAN Draw a picture of your new scene. Include yourself as one of the characters.

WRITE Now write your short drama. Tell what everyone says and does. Use another sheet of paper if you need it. Remember to:

- Begin with a list of the **characters**.
- Name the place and tell what happens in this **setting**.
- Make the **dialogue** sound like real talking.

Prepare to Read

GENRE STUDY **Dramas** are stories that are read and acted out.

MAKE A PREDICTION Preview **Mount Rushmore**. You know that dramas have a cast of characters, dialogue, and a setting. Use these to help you predict. What do you think will happen?

SET A PURPOSE Read to find out what the kids do on a class trip and to see if your prediction is right. If not, think about what a drama is like and make a new prediction as you read.

Mount Rushmore

READ Describe the setting where the drama takes place.

Cast: Mrs. Todd Dan Mr. Rick Roz

Mrs. Todd: Here we are at Mount Rushmore!

Dan: Wow! Look at the four big presidents!

Mr. Rick: Class, tell me what you know about the presidents you see in the rocks. ▶

Close Reading Tip

Is your prediction right so far? If not, think about the genre and make a new prediction.

CHECK MY UNDERSTANDING

Who are the characters in the drama?

READ What are the characters like? Use details from the dialogue and pictures to describe them. Tell why they act the way they do.

Roz: George Washington is one of the presidents. He was our first president.

Dan: I see Abraham Lincoln. He wanted all people to be free.

Mr. Rick: What about the other presidents?

Roz and Dan: Um. . . .

Mrs. Todd: I know what we will do back at school. Find out more about the presidents!

Close Reading Tip

Mark important ideas with *.

CHECK MY UNDERSTANDING

Why do Roz and Dan say "Um"?

Cite Text Evidence

WRITE ABOUT IT You used what you know about the characters, dialogue, and setting to help you make predictions. Did your predictions match what happened in the drama? Write to tell what you were right about. Tell what happened differently.

Guided Practice

READ Together

Prepare to Read

GENRE STUDY **Opinion writing** tells an author's thoughts, beliefs, or ideas about a topic. Look for:

- ways the author tries to make the reader agree with him or her
- reasons that support an opinion

SET A PURPOSE Think about the author's words as you read. Then decide, or **evaluate**, which details are the most important to help you understand the text.

POWER WORDS
contest
liberty
hope

Meet Libby Martinez.

The Contest

by Libby Martinez
illustrated by Nina de Polonia

America has many symbols. A symbol stands for something. A symbol can be a flag. It can be a statue. It can also be a bird!

Find out about symbols that some students like best. Who gives the best reasons? It is a contest. Vote for your favorite symbol!

Eagle

The eagle is the best American symbol because eagles are brave. They make their nests in very tall trees or on cliffs. They keep their babies safe.

The eagle is also the best because it is strong. Eagles have very strong wings. They can fly 10,000 feet in the air! The eagle is brave and strong, like America.

Washington Monument
George Washington was the first president. There are many monuments to honor him. He is on Mount Rushmore with three other presidents. His face is 60 feet tall!
George Washington
Mount Rushmore
Pete
Washington Monument
But I think the Washington Monument is better. It honors just George Washington. It is 555 feet tall. It is the best symbol because it looks like a big number 1! That stands for our first president!

Washington Monument

George Washington was the first president. There are many monuments to honor him. He is on Mount Rushmore with three other presidents. His face is 60 feet tall!

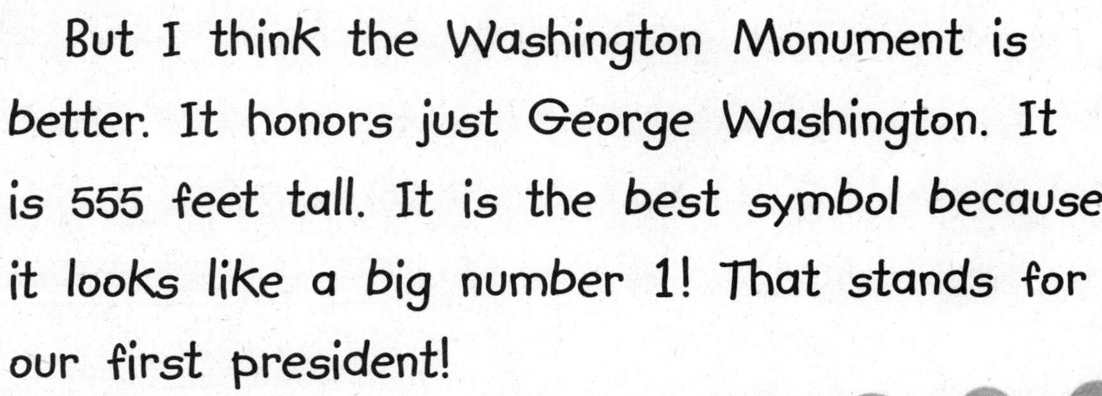

But I think the Washington Monument is better. It honors just George Washington. It is 555 feet tall. It is the *best symbol* because it looks like a big number 1! That stands for our first president!

Statue of Liberty

My favorite symbol is the Statue of Liberty. I like it because liberty means freedom. Many people come to America to be free. They hope for a better life.

France gave America the statue. That is another reason I like it. I like that countries can give gifts to one another. The Statue of Liberty makes me think of hope and friends.

Lincoln Memorial

The Lincoln Memorial is the best symbol. First, it stands for freedom. It was made to honor President Abraham Lincoln. He said all people should be free.

Lincoln Memorial

Second, Dr. Martin Luther King, Jr., gave a famous speech there. It was about being fair to all people. The Lincoln Memorial stands for being free and fair.

The Flag

The best symbol is the flag. I like it because it stands for our whole country. The 50 stars stand for the 50 states.

Brad

I also like the flag because it tells us about our past. Long ago, there were just 13 states. They were called colonies at first. The 13 stripes stand for the first 13 states.

Now vote! Which symbol do you like best? Why?

Respond to Reading

Use details from **The Contest** to answer these questions with a partner.

1. **Evaluate** Jade says that eagles are brave. Is this a detail that helps you understand why the eagle is a good symbol? Tell why or why not.

2. Which character gives the best reasons for his or her opinion? Tell why you think so.

Listening Tip

Listen carefully to your partner. Think of what you agree with and do not agree with.

Cite Text Evidence

READ Together

Write an Opinion

PROMPT Which American symbol from **The Contest** do you like best? Why? Use details from the text and your own ideas to explain.

PLAN Write the name of your favorite symbol. Write reasons why you like it.

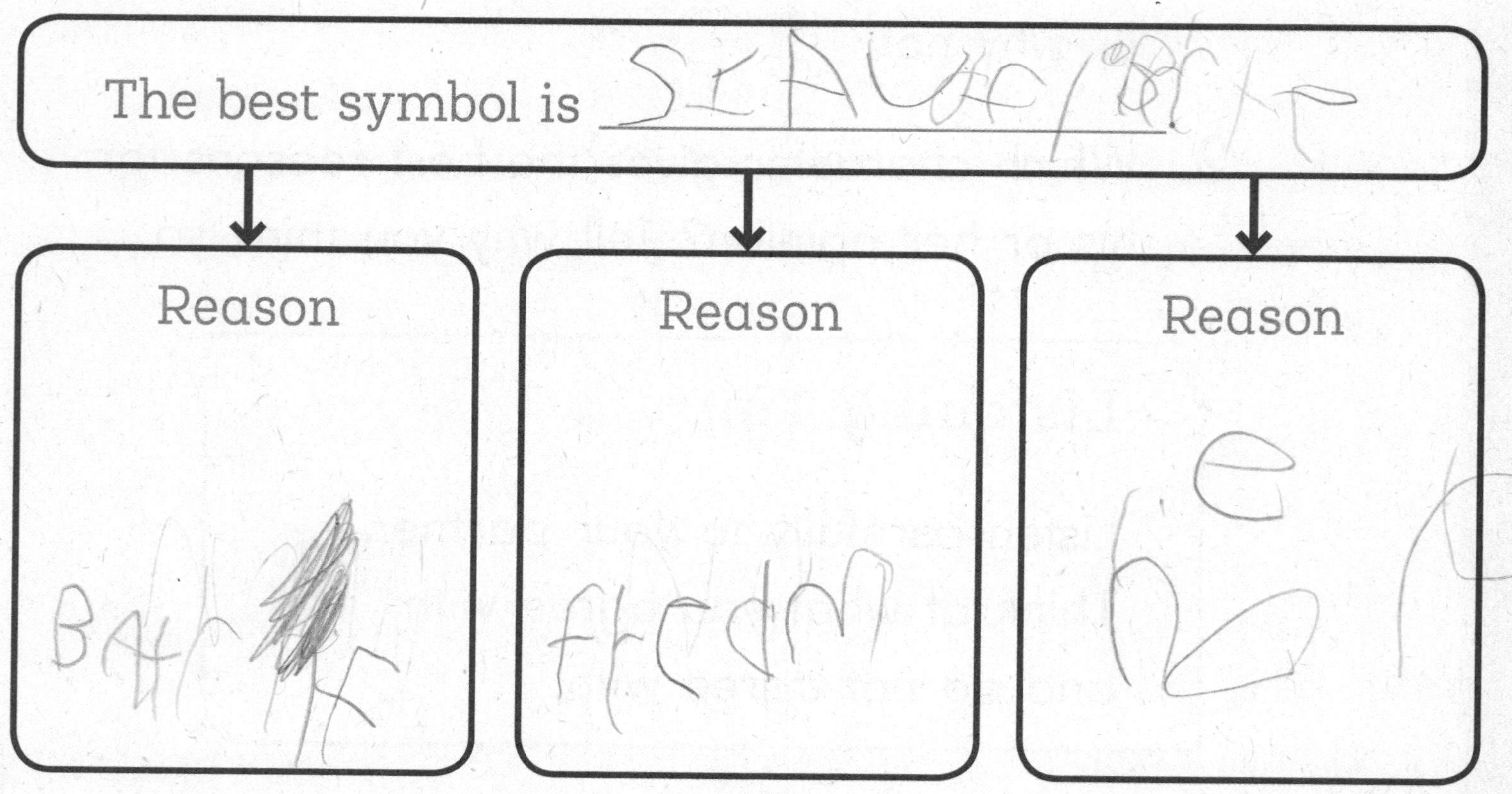

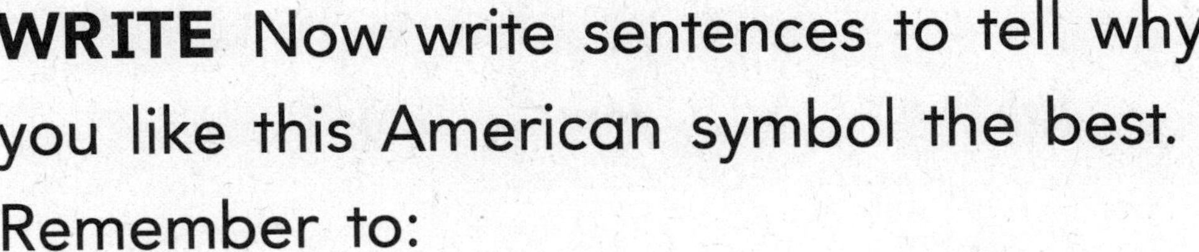

WRITE Now write sentences to tell why you like this American symbol the best. Remember to:

- Tell your opinion.
- Use the word **because** to make your reasons clear.

I likfredma

Prepare to Read

GENRE STUDY **Opinion writing** tells an author's thoughts, beliefs, or ideas about a topic.

MAKE A PREDICTION Preview **A Great Day**. It tells about George Washington. What do you think you will learn?

SET A PURPOSE Read to find out an author's opinion of George Washington. Find reasons the author gives to explain that opinion.

A Great Day

READ What does the author want you to think of George Washington?

We have a special day to honor George Washington. I think that is a great idea! He was one of the great people in our country's past. Long ago, George Washington led the army for America. He helped our country win its freedom. ▶

Close Reading Tip

Circle words you don't know. Then figure them out.

CHECK MY UNDERSTANDING

What is one reason that George Washington is great?

READ Underline more reasons the author gives for why George Washington is great. How does including many reasons in the text help you understand the author's opinion?

Close Reading Tip

Mark important ideas with a *.

George Washington helped start our country. Some people wanted him to be king. But he did not think it was a good idea for the country to have a king. So George Washington was our first president.

It is great to have a day to honor George Washington. It is called Presidents' Day! Abraham Lincoln is also honored on that day. We think about how the presidents helped us long ago.

CHECK MY UNDERSTANDING

What do you think is the best reason the author gives for remembering George Washington?

Cite Text Evidence

WRITE ABOUT IT Why did the author write **A Great Day**? Do you agree with the author's opinion? Tell why or why not.

Guided Practice

Prepare to Read

GENRE STUDY **Informational text** is nonfiction. It gives facts about a topic. Look for:

- photographs
- headings that stand out
- the order of events

POWER WORDS

national

towers

base

SET A PURPOSE As you read, **make connections** by finding ways that this text is like things in your life and other texts you have read. This will help you understand and remember the text.

Build Background: American Symbols

THE STATUE OF LIBERTY

by Tyler Monroe

A National Symbol

The Statue of Liberty is a symbol of American freedom.
The statue is of a woman holding a tablet and a torch.

The torch and tablet stand for different things. The torch means she is bringing the light of freedom to the world. The tablet stands for the United States' laws.

The statue is on Liberty Island in New York Harbor. The statue is made of steel and copper. The torch towers more than 300 feet (91 meters) above the ground.

A Gift from France

France gave the Statue of Liberty to the United States. It was a gift of friendship. The statue was designed by Frédéric Auguste Bartholdi.

Frédéric Auguste Bartholdi

Workers began building the statue in Paris, France, in 1875. It was ready to send to the United States in 1884.

The statue was too big to send in one piece. Workers took it apart and shipped it in 214 crates. The statue and the base it stands on were finished in 1886.

The Symbol Then and Now

For many years, immigrants came to America by ship. The ships passed the Statue of Liberty. The statue welcomed people to the United States.

Over time weather hurt the Statue of Liberty. By the 1980s repairs were needed. The statue was cleaned inside and out. A new torch was made.

Millions of people visit the Statue of Liberty each year. Visitors go inside the statue. They can climb 354 steps to look out of the crown on her head.

Use details from **The Statue of Liberty** to answer these questions with a partner.

1. **Make Connections** Both **The Statue of Liberty** and **The Contest** tell about the Statue of Liberty. How are the two texts alike? How are they different?

2. What part of **The Statue of Liberty** reminds you of your own life? Explain why.

Talking Tip

Wait for your turn to speak. Then explain your ideas and feelings clearly.

I think _____ because _____.

Cite Text Evidence

Write an Ad

PROMPT Why should people visit the Statue of Liberty? Write an ad to make people want to go there. Use facts from **The Statue of Liberty** in your reasons.

PLAN First, draw and write notes about your favorite facts that you learned.

Statue of Liberty

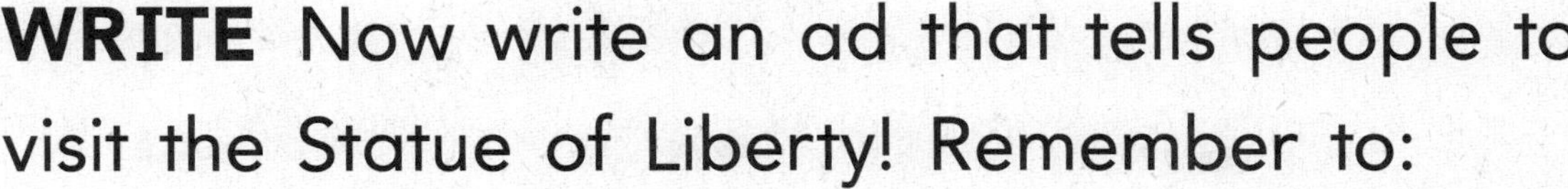

WRITE Now write an ad that tells people to visit the Statue of Liberty! Remember to:

- Tell what the statue stands for.
- Use describing words and give good reasons to make people really want to go there.

On My Own

Prepare to Read

GENRE STUDY **Informational text** is nonfiction. It gives facts about a topic.

MAKE A PREDICTION Preview **The Plant Doctor.** This text tells about a famous American. What do you think you will learn about him?

SET A PURPOSE Read to find out who the famous person is. Find clues in the words and pictures that the text is organized to first describe one part of his life and then another part.

The Plant Doctor

READ The author describes a boy named George. What is he like?

Once there was a boy who loved plants. He had a garden. If a plant did not grow, he found out why and helped it. Soon, neighbors asked him for help. They called him the plant doctor! But his real name was George Washington Carver. ▶

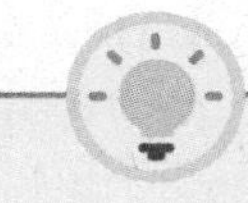

Close Reading Tip

Mark important ideas with *.

CHECK MY UNDERSTANDING

When George was little, he was good at

Close Reading Tip

Put a **?** by the parts you have questions about.

READ What did George do when he grew up?

George loved school, and after he grew up, he still went to school. He found out all about plants. He helped farmers grow plants better. He found out how to make all kinds of things from plants, too. He was happy to help others and teach them about plants.

The George Washington Carver National Monument was made to honor him. You can go there to find out about this great man.

CHECK MY UNDERSTANDING

The author describes George as a child and then as a grown-up. How does this help you learn about him?

Cite Text Evidence

WRITE ABOUT IT How are **The Statue of Liberty** and **The Plant Doctor** alike? Write sentences to explain. Use details from the two texts.

Guided Practice

READ Together

Prepare to Read

GENRE STUDY **Realistic fiction** stories are made up but could happen in real life. Look for:

- a problem, main events, and a resolution
- characters who act and talk like real people

SET A PURPOSE Make pictures in your mind as you read. Words that tell how things look, sound, feel, taste, or smell and words about feelings help you **create mental images**.

POWER WORDS
celebrate
share
tradition
parade
Constitution

Meet Pat Cummings.

HOORAY for HOLIDAYS!

by Pat Cummings

illustrated by John Herzog

"Today we will make holiday cards," said Mrs. Rose. "Holidays are special days we celebrate. Make cards for holidays you like."

"I like the Fourth of July," said Hope. "I will draw stars. They stand for the brave people who made America free."

"Add fireworks!" said Ana.

“My card is for Baby Day,” said Dave.

“There is no Baby Day!” said Hope.

“Mother’s Day is a real holiday. Father’s Day is, too,” said Ana.

“This holiday is for my hamster, Baby!”

"We will help you pick a better holiday, Dave," said Hope. "I vote for New Year's Day. It is the first day of the year."

"Other holidays honor people," said Mike. "My card shows a great man. He wanted all people to treat one another well."

Dr. Martin Luther King, Jr.

"Mine is for Presidents' Day," said Ana. "I like that two presidents share one day."

"I like that school is out that day!" said Dave.

"Can you make a Thanksgiving card, Dave?" asked Ana. "You could trace a turkey."

"You could draw the first Thanksgiving!" said Mike.

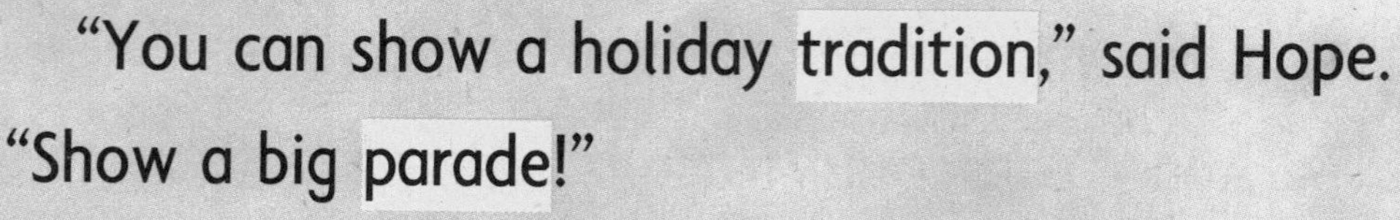

"You can show a holiday tradition," said Hope. "Show a big parade!"

"Make a card to honor workers," said Mike. "Draw people doing different jobs."

Chinese New Year

"Make a Constitution Day card," said Hope. "That day reminds us that we are *all* Americans."

"Even if we seem different," Ana added with a grin. "You can make a big flag."

"Make it red, white, and blue," said Mike.

“I picked my holiday!” Dave said. “It celebrates the end of winter.”

“Is it May Day?” asked Hope and Ana.

Dave’s face lit up with a big smile. He held up his card.

Respond to Reading

Use details from **Hooray for Holidays!** to answer these questions with a partner.

1. **Create Mental Images** Which words help you imagine the holidays the cards show and how the children feel?

2. Did Dave finally pick a good holiday for his card? Give reasons why or why not.

Talking Tip

Add your own idea to what your partner says. Be polite.

I like your idea.
My idea is ________________.

Write a Holiday Card

PROMPT Pick one of the holidays from **Hooray for Holidays!** Make a holiday card. Use details from the story for ideas.

PLAN First, draw the front of your card. Show what your holiday is about.

WRITE Now write the message you want to say in your holiday card. Then share it with classmates. Remember to:

- Write the name of the holiday correctly.
- Include facts about the holiday.

Prepare to Read

GENRE STUDY **Realistic fiction** stories are made up but could happen in real life.

MAKE A PREDICTION Preview **Arbor Day**. You know that stories have a problem that gets solved. What do you think the problem is in this story?

SET A PURPOSE Read to find out what a group of people does to solve a problem on Arbor Day.

Arbor Day

READ Describe the problem the neighbors have.

The neighbors want to plant a tree to celebrate Arbor Day. Where can they plant it? There is a big, empty lot in the neighborhood. But, it is full of gray rocks. There are piles of trash and no grass. The lot is a big, dusty mess!

"We can clean up the lot!" the kids say. ▶

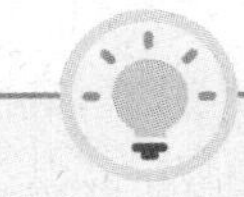

Close Reading Tip

Underline the important describing words.

CHECK MY UNDERSTANDING

What are some of the words the author uses to help you make a picture in your mind of the empty lot?

READ Describe the main events that happen and the resolution, or how the neighbors solve the problem.

The kids rake up rocks. Everyone puts trash in bags. They plant grass and flowers. "Now we have to plant the tree!" the kids say. And they do.

The lot is not empty now. The neighbors enjoy a picnic by the new tree. "Did you know that **arbor** means **tree**?" Jen calls out.

"So *that's* why we planted a tree today!" the kids say. "Happy Arbor Day!"

Close Reading Tip

Did your prediction match what happened in the story? What were you right about? What was different?

CHECK MY UNDERSTANDING

Did the author write this story to entertain you or to give facts? Tell how you know.

Cite Text Evidence

WRITE ABOUT IT What happens at the picnic? Think of a new problem the neighbors have. How do they solve it? Write about the story events in order. Draw a picture on another sheet of paper.

Guided Practice

Prepare to Read

GENRE STUDY **Poetry** uses images, sounds, and rhythm to express ideas and feelings. Look for:

- rhyme, or words whose endings sound alike
- rhythm, or pattern of beats from the words
- words that make you think of powerful images or pictures

SET A PURPOSE As you read, listen for the rhyming words and the rhythm, or beat, the words make. Use describing words and other details to help you understand the ideas and feelings you get from the poems.

Meet Kristine O'Connell George.

Patriotic Poems

illustrated by Amanda Lima

Yankee Doodle

Yankee Doodle came to town,
Riding on a pony;
Stuck a feather in his hat
And called it Macaroni.

Traditional Song

Labor Day

First Monday in September
that's when we remember
to honor workers who toil long.
Their efforts make our country strong.
We give a gift they all like best;
We give them all a day of rest!

Marci Ridlon

A Day for Martin Luther King, Jr.

We hear the words "let freedom ring!"
And think of Martin Luther King.

A man of honor, standing tall
Dreamed of equality for all.

He saw a world where there could be,
All people living proud and free.

Today we celebrate and sing,
So here and now, let freedom ring!

Kate Arnold

Celebration

Wait here a minute,
  I'll bring your gifts—
  ribbons for your branches,
  buckets of water, and
  a wheelbarrow of mulch.

Happy Arbor Day!

Kristine O'Connell George

Use details from **Patriotic Poems** to answer these questions with a partner.

1. **Elements of Poetry** How do each of the poems make you feel? How do the describing words and the rhyme and rhythm help make you feel that way?

2. Why do you think each poem was written? Give reasons.

Listening Tip

Listen carefully. Make connections. How is what your partner says like other things you know?

READ Together

Let's Wrap Up!

Essential Question

What do holidays and symbols tell about our country?

Pick one of these activities to show what you have learned about the topic.

1. A Symbol for You

Think about the American symbols you have read about. Make a symbol that stands for you! It can show something that is important to you. Explain it to a partner.

2. America's Parade

Draw a parade to celebrate America. Which famous Americans will march by? Which monuments will be on floats? Add labels. Tell your class about the parade!

Word Challenge

Can you use the word participate to tell about your parade?

My Notes

Glossary

A

able If you are able to do something, you can do it. She is **able** to skate.

appreciate When you appreciate something, you are thankful for it. After I work hard, I **appreciate** resting.

B

base The base of something is the bottom part of it. The fountain is on a **base** made of stone.

blackout A blackout is when the electricity stops working and all the lights go out. We had to use a flashlight to see during the **blackout**.

busy When you are busy, you have lots of things to do. Are you too **busy** to sit down and rest?

C

celebrate When you celebrate, you do something fun to remember a special event. Let's have a party to **celebrate** your birthday!

Constitution The Constitution is the group of laws that we follow in our country.

The **Constitution** tells us what we can and cannot do.

contest A contest is a game or race in which people try to win. She got a prize for winning the **contest**.

D

duty A duty is something that you should do. A doctor's **duty** is to help sick people get well.

F

faces If something faces you, the front part of it is toward you. The house **faces** the sea.

fades When something fades, it slowly loses color and goes away. The light **fades** after the sun goes down.

freedom Freedom is being able to do what you want to do. At the park, we have the **freedom** to run around.

G

groan A groan is a deep sound you make when you are hurt or not happy. He said "**Groan!**" when Mom told him to clean his room.

grouchy When you are grouchy, you are in a bad mood. I feel **grouchy** when I do not get enough sleep.

H

hope When you hope for something, you wish for it to happen. I **hope** I will go camping soon.

huddled If a group of people is huddled, they are very close together. We **huddled** with the coach so we could talk about the game.

I

idea When you have an idea, you are thinking about something. My great **idea** for having fun is to ride bikes.

L

liberty When you have liberty, you can live your life the way you want. We have the **liberty** to go to any town we choose.

M

monuments Monuments are statues or buildings that help us remember a person or event. The Washington Monument is one of my favorite **monuments**.

N

national If something is national, it belongs to the whole country. Our country has many **national** symbols, like the eagle and the flag.

normal When things are normal, they are like they usually are. It is **normal** for it to be hot in the summer.

O

orbit When things orbit, they move around something in a circle. Planets **orbit** around the sun.

P

parade A parade is a group of people who march or ride down a street on a special day. We clapped to the music as the **parade** went by.

participate When you participate, you take part in doing something. All the kids **participate** in the game.

pattern A pattern is something that happens over and over again. The days of the week follow a **pattern**.

period A period is an amount of time. It was rainy for a **period** of a few days.

S

scene A scene is a part of a play. The first **scene** in the play takes place on a farm.

seasons Seasons are the four parts of a year—spring, summer, fall, and winter. I like summer better than the other **seasons**.

share When two people share something, they both have it or use it. It is nice to **share** toys and other things with your friends.

shines When something shines, it gives off a bright light. The flashlight **shines** and lights up the dark room.

sights Sights are interesting places people like to visit. We saw the park and other **sights** in the city.

solar If something is solar, it has to do with the sun. **Solar** power is made from sunlight.

still When a place is still, it is quiet. The house is very **still** late at night.

symbol A symbol is something that is used to mean something else. A heart is a **symbol** of love.

T

towers If a one thing towers over something else, it is a lot taller. The tall building **towers** over the smaller buildings.

tradition A tradition is a special way people have done something for a long time. Is it your family's **tradition** to have a big meal on Thanksgiving?

W

wait When you wait, you stay ready for something you think will happen. **Wait** for the green light, and then cross the street.

wasted If something is wasted, it is not used in a smart way. I **wasted** water when I left it on too long by mistake.

weather The weather is what the air outside is like. The **weather** was too cold and rainy to go outside.

worth If one thing is worth the same as another thing, it is just as good, important, or useful. The nice shirt is **worth** the money I paid for it.

Index of Titles and Authors

Acknowledgments

Blackout by John Rocco. Copyright © 2011 by John Rocco. Reprinted by permission of Hyperion Books, an imprint of Disney Books Group and Tramuntana Editorial.

"Celebration" from *Old Elm Speaks: Tree Poems* by Kristine O'Connell George. Text copyright © 1998 by Kristine O'Connell George. Reprinted by permission of Houghton Mifflin Harcourt and Kristine O'Connell George.

Day and Night by Margaret Hall. Text copyright © 2007 by Capstone Press. Reprinted by permission of Capstone Press Publishers.

"Labor Day" by Marci Ridlon from *Days to Celebrate* by Lee Bennett Hopkins. Published by Greenwillow Books, an imprint of HarperCollins Publishers. Text copyright © 2004 by Marci Ridlon. Reprinted by permission of Marci Ridlon McGill.

The Statue of Liberty by Tyler Monroe. Text copyright © 2014 by Capstone Press, a Capstone imprint. Reprinted by permission of Capstone Press Publishers.

Waiting Is Not Easy! by Mo Willems. Copyright © 2014 by Mo Willems. First published by Hyperion Books for Children, an imprint of Disney Publishing. Reprinted by permission of Disney Book Group and Wernick & Pratt Agency on behalf of the author.

Credits

4 (b) ©imagenavi/Getty Images; 4 (b) ©Mikhail Kokhanchikov/iStockPhoto; 4 (tl) ©Zurijeta/Shutterstock; 4 (bl) ©imagenavi/Getty Images, ©Mikhail Kokhanchikov/iStockPhoto; 5 (b) ©Jib Jab Bros. Studios; 5 (b) ©Jib Jab Bros. Studios; 5 (tl), (tl) ©Houghton Mifflin Harcourt, (br) ©Houghton Mifflin Harcourt, (tl) (bg) ©nycshooter/iStock/Getty Images Plus/Getty Images, (bl) ©Nina Crews; 6 (tl), (t) ©IIIerlok_Xolms/Shutterstock, (c) ©Kathryn8/DigitalVision Vectors/Getty Images, (bl) ©Marilyn Nieves/E+/Getty Images, (bc) ©SungheeKang/Shutterstock, (br) ©erikreis/iStock/Getty Images Plus/Getty Images; 7 (t) ©Amy Nichole Harris/Shutterstock; 7 (c) ©Werayuth Tes/Shutterstock; 7 (r) (bg) ©Amy Nichole Harris/Shutterstock, (l) ©Suat Gursozlu/Shutterstock; 8 (c) ©Helena_Ogorodnikova/Shutterstock, (bg) ©Andrew_Mayovskyy/iStock/Getty Images Plus/Getty Images, (r) ©Timothy Herremans/EyeEm/Getty Images; 13 (tl) ©kikovic/Shutterstock; 13 (tr) ©Houghton Mifflin Harcourt; 13 (bl) ©N K/Shutterstock; 13 (br) ©Zurijeta/Shutterstock; 44 ©Standret/iStock/Getty Images Plus; 45 (bl) ©imagenavi/Getty Images, ©Mikhail Kokhanchikov/iStockPhoto; 46 ©age fotostock/Superstock; 47 ©Keith Levit/Shutterstock; 49 ©Michal Zak/Shutterstock; 50 ©Graham Custance Photography/Getty Images; 51 ©Onfokus/iStock Unreleased/Getty Images Plus/Getty Images; 52 ©Jared Hobbs/All Canada Photos/Superstock; 53 ©Romilly Lockyer/The Image Bank/Getty Images; 54 (r) ©Andrey Volkovets/Shutterstock; 54 (l) ©Bobby Dailey/Shutterstock; 54 (t) ©Nancy Tripp/Shutterstock; 54 (b) ©Aleksey Sagitov/Shutterstock; 55 (bl) ©imagenavi/Getty Images, ©Mikhail Kokhanchikov/iStockPhoto; 57 (bl) ©imagenavi/Getty Images, ©Mikhail Kokhanchikov/iStockPhoto; 60 ©John E Marriott/All Canada Photos/Getty Images; 62 (bl) (inset) ©Matthew Septimus; 62 (tl) ©Houghton Mifflin Harcourt, (br) ©Houghton Mifflin Harcourt, (tl) (bg) ©nycshooter/iStock/Getty Images Plus/Getty Images, (bl) ©Nina Crews; 64 (bg) (inset) ©Houghton Mifflin Harcourt, (bg) ©bibi57/E+/Getty Images, ©Kimberly Sue Walker/iStock/Getty Images Plus, ©Predrag Vuckovic/E+/Getty Images; 64 (tl) ©Nina Crews; 65 (r) ©Nina Crews; 66 (bg) ©tbradford/iStock/Getty Images Plus/Getty Images, (tl) ©Nina Crews, (bl) ©Nina Crews; 67 (bg) ©Peter Steiner/Alamy, (b) ©Nina Crews; 68 (bg) ©Houghton Mifflin Harcourt, (r) ©cmart7327/iStock/Getty Images Plus/Getty Images, (c) ©Nina Crews; 70 (c) ©Houghton Mifflin Harcourt, (bl) ©Nina Crews, (br) ©Nina Crews, (bg) ©Nina Crews, (cl) ©Nina Crews, (tr) ©Nina Crews; 72 (c) ©Nadezhda1906/iStock/Getty Images Plus/Getty Images, (cl) ©varandah/Shutterstock, (bl) ©Nina Crews; 73 (l) ©Stevica Mrdja/iStock/Getty Images Plus/Getty Images, (cr) ©Orange Stock Photo Production Inc./Alamy, (bg) ©Nina Crews; 74 (insets) ©fergregory/iStock/Getty Images Plus/Getty Images, (c) ©Houghton Mifflin Harcourt, (bg) ©Nina Crews; 76 (l) ©Houghton Mifflin Harcourt, (r) ©Houghton Mifflin Harcourt, (bg) (l) ©Nina Crews, (bg) (r) ©Nina Crews; 77 (tl) ©Houghton Mifflin Harcourt, (br) ©Houghton Mifflin Harcourt, (tl) (bg) ©nycshooter/iStock/Getty Images Plus/Getty Images, (bl) ©Nina Crews; 79 (tl) ©Houghton Mifflin Harcourt, (br) ©Houghton Mifflin Harcourt, (tl) (bg) ©nycshooter/iStock/Getty Images Plus/Getty Images, (bl) ©Nina Crews; 118 ©cigdem/Shutterstock; 119 ©Jib Jab Bros. Studios; 119 ©Jib Jab Bros. Studios; 120 ©Jib Jab Media Inc.; 122 ©Tania Kolinko/Shutterstock; 123 ©Elena Zajchikova/Shutterstock; 124 ©S. Noree Saisalam/Shutterstock; 125 (inset) ©ayelet-keshet/Shutterstock; 128 (bg) ©IIIerlok_Xolms/Shutterstock; 128 (inset) ©Kathryn8/DigitalVision Vectors/Getty Images; 128 (t) ©IIIerlok_Xolms/Shutterstock, (c) ©Kathryn8/DigitalVision Vectors/Getty Images, (bl) ©Marilyn Nieves/E+/Getty Images, (bc) ©SungheeKang/Shutterstock, (br) ©erikreis/iStock/Getty Images Plus/Getty Images; 128 (bg) ©s_maria/Shutterstock; 130 (bl) ©Larry French/Houghton Mifflin Harcourt; 160 ©Libby Martinez; 162 (tl) ©Ron Chapple/Corbis; 162 (tc) @Eyewire/Getty Images; 162 (tr) ©kuosumo/Fotolia; 162 (bl) ©Ocean/Corbis; 162 (bc) ©tab1962/iStock/Getty; 162 (br) ©Jupiterimages/Brand X Pictures/Alamy Images; 163 (inset) ©compassandcamera/E+/Getty Images; 163 (inset) ©Jerry Amster/SuperStock; 163 (tc) @Eyewire/Getty Images; 163 (bl) ©Ocean/Corbis; 163 (tr) ©kuosumo/Fotolia; 170 (inset) ©LarryHerfindal/Getty Images; 170 (inset) ©compassandcamera/E+/Getty Images; 171 (r) ©AFP/Getty Images; 171 (l) ©Bettmann/Getty Images; 172 (b) ©MarkWagonerProductions/iStock/Getty Images Plus/Getty Images; 172 (t) ©Chuck Liddy/AP Images; 173 (inset) ©Jerry Amster/SuperStock; 182 ©Ron Chapple/Corbis; 183 (r) (bg) ©Amy Nichole Harris/Shutterstock, (l) ©Suat

Gursozlu/Shutterstock; 184 (bg) ©Suat Gursozlu/Shutterstock; 184 (fg) ©ErickN/Shutterstock; 185 ©Amy Nichole Harris/Shutterstock; 186 ©iofoto/Shutterstock; 187 (b) ©North Wind Picture Archives/Alamy; 187 (inset) ©Library of Congress Prints & Photographs Division; 187 (bg) ©Suat Gursozlu/Shutterstock; 188 ©Library of Congress Prints & Photographs Division; 188 (bg) ©Suat Gursozlu/Shutterstock; 189 ©North Wind Picture Archives/Alamy; 190 ©Bettmann/Getty Images; 191 (fg) ©Library of Congress Prints & Photographs Division; 191 (bg) ©Suat Gursozlu/Shutterstock; 192 ©FORRAY Didier/sagaphoto.com/Alamy; 193 (r) (bg) ©Amy Nichole Harris/Shutterstock, (l) ©Suat Gursozlu/Shutterstock; 195 (r) (bg) ©Amy Nichole Harris/Shutterstock, (l) ©Suat Gursozlu/Shutterstock; 198 ©Corbis Historical/Getty Images; 200 ©Barbara Cummings; 200 ©Werayuth Tes/Shutterstock; 202 (fg) ©Poznyakov/Shutterstock; 202 (t) ©Robert Kneschke/Shutterstock; 203 ©Tomwang112/iStock/Getty Images Plus/Getty Images; 204 (fg) ©SerrNovik/Dreamstime; 205 ©onajourney/Shutterstock; 206 ©Houghton Mifflin Harcourt; 206 ©Jaromir Urbanek/Shutterstock; 207 (bg) ©aimintang/E+/Getty Images; 207 (inset) ©Georgina198/Shutterstock; 208 ©Shutterstock; 209 (bg) ©Jaromir Urbanek/Shutterstock; 209 (inset) ©Olga Kovalenko/Shutterstock; 210 ©legna69/iStock/Getty Images Plus/Getty Images; 211 (tr) ©Werayuth Tes/Shutterstock; 213 (tr) ©Werayuth Tes/Shutterstock; 218 ©Brian Rooney/R7 Media; 226 ©Andrey Popov/Shutterstock; 226 (inset) ©Best Vector Elements/Shutterstock; 227 ©Africa Studio/Shutterstock